LET THAT SH*T GO

A JOURNAL FOR LEAVING YOUR BULLSH*T BEHIND AND CREATING A HAPPY LIFE

· monica sweeney ·

Castle Point Books
New York

www.stmartins.com
www.castlepointbooks.com

The Castle Point Books trademark is owned by
Castle Point Publications, LLC.
Castle Point books are published and distributed by
St. Martin's Press.

ISBN 978-1-250-18190-9 (trade paperback)

Design by Katie Jennings Campbell
Production by Tara Long

Images used under license by Shutterstock.com

Our books may be purchased in bulk for promotional,
educational, or business use. Please contact your local
bookseller or the Macmillan Corporate and Premium Sales
Department at 1-800-221-7945, extension 5442, or by e-mail
at MacmillanSpecialMarkets@macmillan.com.

First Edition: July 2018

OH, HELLO!

WELCOME TO YOUR TRUE SELF! This person is delightful as fuck, because he or she doesn't give a crap about the bullshit, believes good energy begets more good energy, and imagines a place where a dash of silliness, a dose of heart, and a heavy sprinkling of profanity are as healthy a lifestyle recipe as any. Forget about harboring grudges, keeping score, and feeling the annoying weight of everyone else's garbage. Instead, take a detour around that destructive route of reckoning and navigate your way to a scenic little street of serenity.

On the pages of this journal, you'll find opportunities to tip your hat and say, *Adieu, motherfucker!* to the negative things in your life, and welcome in the positive reflections and happy moments that await you. Get all up in your emotive self with a shit-ton of cheerfully irreverent activities—whether in order or by hopping around—and relish the gentle catharsis of not giving a fuck.

ENJOY THESE REFLECTIONS AND GIVE YOUR SOUL A NICE FUCKING BOOST.

OFF TO THE RACES

Straight out of the gate, write down the things that make you feel like crap! Use pencil or a light-colored writing utensil.

Now, with bright colored pencils, sparkly gel pens, or bold markers, write over those shitty things with things that make you feel super thrilled. Take a few minutes to focus on those bright colors and bold, positive words. Don't pretend that the bad ones aren't there, but let yourself bring the good ones front and center.

CA-CAW, MOTHERFUCKER

There are things in this world that feel overwhelming, that engulf us with emotion, and that burn us out. Well rise up from those ashes, my fine friend. Think of three ways you can be a magical bird of metamorphosis, and fly like the beautiful fucking phoenix that you are.

4

"LOOK WHERE YOU'RE GOING, NOT WHERE YOU'VE BEEN."

—MY MOM

*(The most influential mantra of
my adult life was invented because I
bumped into a lot of shit as a child.)*

STOP DWELLING ON THE PAST

If you keep staring back at it, you'll miss all of the amazing things in front of you (or slam the fuck into them). What are things you want to see on the road ahead?

TREAT YOURSELF

When you're feeling shitty—whether it's from a bad day, a crummy immune system, or just enduring the slow crawl of human existence—it's time to do something special to take your mind off things. Feel like sitting in a bubble bath and speaking to no one? Great! Want to go for a hike and see some happy little trees? Get at it! Call it me-time, call it self-care, or call it getting fancy as fuck.

Carve out some time to treat yourself like royalty. Reserve three days over the next three months, jot down what you'll do, and make that shit happen.

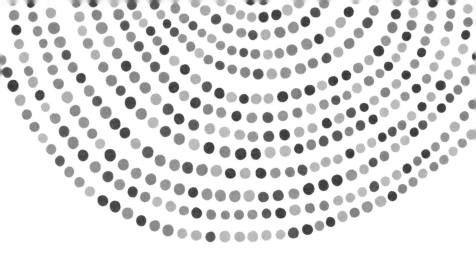

SCHA·DEN·FREU·DE
ˈSHÄDƏN-FROIDƏ/

noun

1. *pleasure derived by someone from another person's misfortune.*

SHADY SCHADENFREUDE

Sometimes when you're angry or hurt, it feels best to wrap yourself in a snuggly quilt of schadenfreude—to feel that warm reassurance that one day karma will circle back, give all fuck-heads what they deserve, and reveal that some of the most smug people you know are only pretending to be happy.

You know what's also great? Not giving a fuck. The longer you spend quilting a patchwork of hopes and dreams for someone else's demise, the less time you'll have to sew your own happiness. Make a quilt of the things that make you happy. Imagine what it would be made of for the next few minutes and snuggle in!

NON-PLATITUDES ON GRATITUDE

True Gratitude is subtle and unassuming. Not to be confused with her attention-seeking little sister, #Blessed, Gratitude is the heart of the mindfulness family, and she's not here for anyone's phony shit. If you were Gratitude, how would you express yourself in a meaningful way?

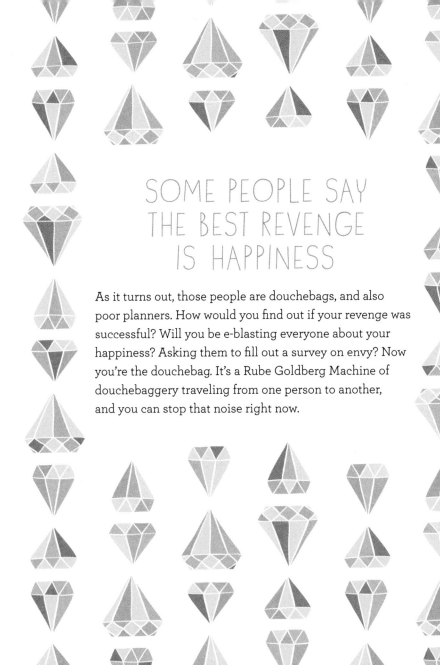

SOME PEOPLE SAY THE BEST REVENGE IS HAPPINESS

As it turns out, those people are douchebags, and also poor planners. How would you find out if your revenge was successful? Will you be e-blasting everyone about your happiness? Asking them to fill out a survey on envy? Now you're the douchebag. It's a Rube Goldberg Machine of douchebaggery traveling from one person to another, and you can stop that noise right now.

Instead, consider ditching revenge and spreading your happiness. What are five ways you can put someone else's happiness in motion?

CAREENING CAREER

Sometimes problems at work can make you feel as if you're flying off the rails. Whether it's something large or small, a person or a project, it's helpful to take things into a lower gear and approach the issue slowly.

What are a few things that drive you nuts at work?

How could you slow down, take a breath, and approach it in a productive way?

FILTERED AS FUCK

Every once in a while, when you're reacting to a situation, the first words out of your mouth, your texting thumbs, or your keyboard feel super cathartic to say in the moment, but are actually dumb as fuck and will only make the situation worse.

Instead of offering the potent version of what you wanted to say, how could you water it down? Can you take a pause, filter your reaction through a nice little mesh of composure, and come out with something of value?

What I Wanted to Say

....

....

....

Likely Result

....

....

....

What I Should Say

....

....

....

Hopeful Result

....

....

....

DRIP DROP, AND
YOU DON'T STOP

Poisoning your own thoughts and emotions is easy to do, and frequently starts with just a slow drip of self-doubt. The more often you allow thoughts like "I'm not lovable," "I'm not successful enough," or "I'll never be good at spelunking," to seep into your everyday pool of emotion, you'll suddenly find that the whole fucking well is poisoned.

Write out a list of some of these negative emotional
thoughts:

....

....

....

....

....

....

Now, cross those motherfuckers out. Replace those negative
thoughts with true positive statements about yourself:

....

....

....

....

....

....

NOT TODAY, SATAN!

You can wake up in the morning and let the big bad demons in your life take over, or you can put on your special cape of positivity and power your way above, below, around, or through them.

When have the first thoughts of your day given you anxiety?

_____

_____

_____

_____

_____

_____

_____

What are positive thoughts that can help you blast the
fuck through them?

_____

_____

_____

_____

_____

_____

EAT THE FUCKING ICE CREAM*

Unless you're lactose intolerant

Sometimes, we ruin perfectly good things in the name of innovation or health to make ourselves feel better. Sure, diluting champagne with orange juice and giving it a fun name means you can drink before noon, dumping stale gummy bears onto frozen yogurt helps distract us from the fact that it's not ice cream, and running in those toe sneakers can make you feel more connected to rocks on the ground, but none of these things are as good as the originals and you die a little bit inside while doing them.

What extra efforts do you make to feel virtuous? Are they worth it?

....

....

....

What could you stop trying to fix and just enjoy?

....

....

....

"THERE'S SOMETHING SO
HUMAN ABOUT TAKING
SOMETHING GREAT AND
RUINING IT A LITTLE
SO YOU CAN HAVE
MORE OF IT."

—MICHAEL, *THE GOOD PLACE*

FEELIN' TORCHED

There are always going to be circumstances that lead us into emotional or creative droughts. They dry us up until one day we're just a tinderbox of banality waiting to be lit up in flames. Either water that fucker or roast some marshmallows over the fire.

REHYDRATE THAT SHIT

If you're willing to give what you're already doing another go, what steps can you take to bring it back to life?

....

....

....

....

....

....

BURN IT TO THE GROUND

Time to start fresh! If you're in a dry patch and there's no way but the scorched-earth way, what will you build after the smoke clears?

....

....

....

....

....

....

"FOLLOW YOUR PASSION,
STAY TRUE TO YOURSELF,
NEVER FOLLOW SOMEONE
ELSE'S PATH UNLESS YOU'RE
IN THE WOODS AND YOU'RE
LOST AND YOU SEE A PATH,
THEN BY ALL MEANS YOU
SHOULD FOLLOW THAT."

—ELLEN DEGENERES

IT'S OK TO BE
A SHEEP SOMETIMES

Following your dreams and working hard to reach your goals are some of the most valuable things you can do for yourself. But sometimes, our dreams and our goals can be completely out of touch with reality, we run into bad fucking luck, or we've followed them down a road that turned out to be a dead end. Admitting that it didn't work, knowing when to let it go, and knowing when to take someone else's lead can make all the difference.

What are some good ways you can get down with your sheep-like nature and follow someone's example?

....

....

....

....

....

....

BAAA, MOTHERFUCKER!

ONE JOY A DAY
KEEPS BAD SHIT AWAY

Come back to this page every day for a month. On each day, write one thing that made your life a little more joyful, a little more fruitful, or a little more fucking spectacular. They can be big or small, but each entry will act as a nice reminder that there's always something good to be found.

Examples:
Day 1: I got the job! Day 2: I ate a red Starburst.
Day 3: I Googled the word "askew."

1.	16.
2.	17.
3.	18.
4.	19.
5.	20.
6.	21.
7.	22.
8.	23.
9.	24.
10.	25.
11.	26.
12.	27.
13.	28.
14.	29.
15.	30.

GET SHIT DONE...
EVENTUALLY!

Procrastinating big responsibilities is never ideal, but if you're going to do it, do it positively. Instead of sitting on the couch and wallowing in the abject desperation of your immobility, do something productive that you hate less than what you're avoiding. By the time your house is fucking spotless and you've engendered world peace, you'll feel better about getting to The Thing you actually have to do. Make a list and get your shit together.

POSITIVE PROCRASTINATION

- ☐ ....
- ☐ CLEAN THE HOUSE
- ☐ ....
- ☐ ....
- ☐ DO YOUR FUCKING LAUNDRY
- ☐ VOLUNTEER OR HELP A FRIEND
- ☐ ....
- ☐ ....
- ☐ LEARN A LANGUAGE THAT WILL TAKE YEARS TO MASTER
- ☐ ....
- ☐ ....
- ☐ ....
- ☐ ....
- ☐ ....
- ☐ ....
- ☐ ....
- ☐ ....

HARNESS YOUR INNER CONTROL FREAK

Nobody likes a control freak (until that day when all the control freaks of the world have actually planned everything out for the apocalypse and non-planners are stuck flailing around like idiots), but it doesn't mean that you have to completely stop being one. Use your powers for good!

What are the things you keep trying to control the shit out of, but aren't actually in your power to change?

....

....

....

....

Fuck that! Find something you can actually control. What kinds of positive actions can you take?

....

....

....

....

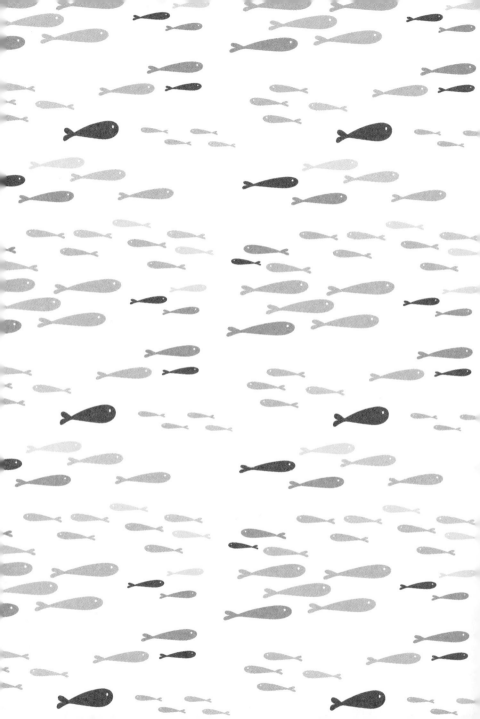

CRAP-TON OF CREEPIN'

Listen, sometimes the search field just accidentally autocompletes the name of your ex, or your ex's new significant other, or your ex's new significant other's dog's social media account. It happens! But staring at photos of other people's lives is only going to make you feel like garbage. Whether it's an ex or a friend whose social media drives you fucking insane, fills you with the ragey kind of envy, or somehow makes you feel a little bit stuck, it's time to cut that shit out. Say it here:

I will not creep on ....

I will not creep on ....

I will not creep on ....

I will not creep on ....

I will not creep on ....

I will not creep on ....

UNDERACHIEVEMENT!

There is something to be said for utter indifference to success. Sure, you can take on responsibilities and be stressed-the-fuck-out forever, or you can take a back seat and see what happens. The cart will probably still move forward. Are there some non-crucial things in your life that you're putting too much effort into, and could cheerfully step away from?

What positives can come from not trying to be on top of everything all the time?

TODAY IS
YOUR FUCKING DAY!

Here, color in something beautiful.
Today is going to be fucking great!

PUMP THE DAMN BRAKES

Functioning on auto-pilot or jumping every time someone tells you to is one of those habits that could use a nice dose of *not-right-fucking-now*. When you're being pulled in a stressful direction, the pace is too fast, or something is starting to deplete your fuel, take a breath and say no.

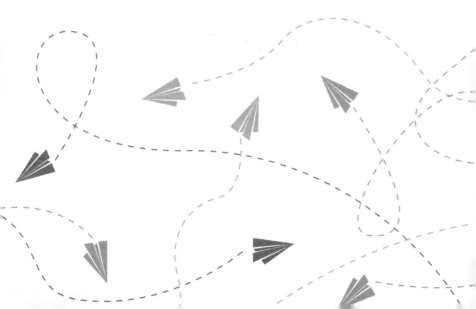

If you took that time for yourself to inhale some fresh, stress-free air instead of the smog from your engines firing on all cylinders, how would it feel? Could you still get where you're going?

EVEN SERIAL KILLERS HAVE MOTHERS WHO LOVE THEM!

Who are the people who show you love? Whether it's through words, gestures, or mere speculation because they're not that great with *feelz*, write down how you know they care.

"OOH, SOMEBODY
LOVES YOU."

—"SOMEBODY LOVES YOU,"
BETTY WHO

THEIR
EMERGENCY
IS NOT
YOUR
EMERGENCY

NOT YOUR FUCKING PROBLEM!

Being helpful and conscientious of others are leading characteristics of people who are not assholes. But being a good person doesn't mean you have to panic, bend over backward, and ruin your own day every time someone else's actions have negative consequences for them.

Don't let someone else's frenzy be your frenzy. Instead of cleaning up their mess for them, how can you take a step back and empower them to do it themselves?

If a flat-out "no" (plus a hard pause where they freak out but you stay chill-as-fuck to stick the landing) just won't work, what are supportive ways you can respond or help without taking on their stress?

CARPE FUCKING DIEM

In this fleeting existence we call life, it'd be a damn shame if you opted out of doing enriching things that were entirely within your reach because you were too scared to try. Whether it's going on that impromptu road trip, making out with that dreamboat across the bar, or doing that EXTREME sport (while also wearing a helmet for...well...all of those things), you have to take advantage of the positive opportunities that present themselves to you.

What's stopped you from taking advantage of these chances in the past?

....

....

....

What moments can you seize the fuck out of in your near future?

....

....

....

"SEIZE THE MOMENT,
'CAUSE TOMORROW YOU
MIGHT BE DEAD."

—BUFFY SUMMERS,
BUFFY THE VAMPIRE SLAYER

CALM AS FUCK

Not to be confused with "stay calm" or "just calm down"—which are phrases uttered only to incite panic or a murderous rage—being calm as fuck is the truest form of tranquility. It's the kind of serenity that turns the flickering neon lights of stress down to gentle sunset hues. Color your way to calm with this happy illustration, and let in the warmth of your new calming light.

"YOUR FEAR OF
LOOKING STUPID
IS HOLDING
YOU BACK."
—RUPAUL

Think of a time when one of your friends acted super fucking goofy, made a scene, and had a blast because they didn't care what the fuck other people thought of them. What about this moment did you like best? What did you appreciate most about them?

....

....

....

....

Now, think of a time when you wanted to act similarly unfettered, but you held yourself back because you thought you'd look dumb. Why did you restrain yourself? How would it have felt to let go?

....

....

....

....

REMEMBER THAT YOU LOVE YOUR
FRIEND *BECAUSE* THEY DIDN'T HOLD
BACK, NOT IN SPITE OF IT.

CALL SOMEBODY WHO GIVES A FUCK

Seriously. You should actually do that. Make time to chat with an old friend, a new friend, or effectively anyone whose voice brings you cozy comfort and shit-tons of joy. Who's on your list of people you keep meaning to reach out to? What do you want to tell them?

TAKE A LOAD OFF

Carrying the extra weight of the rocky parts of your past makes trudging forward feel like an existential CrossFit class that you wish you'd never signed up for. What kinds of stones are you carrying?

....

....

....

Set those stones down gently, paying tribute to the lessons they brought you and the burden you're releasing as you move beyond them. How do you want to leave them? Do you want to linger a bit and tell them to fuck off? Do you want to paint them with the bright colors of their lessons and turn them into happiness rocks? Do it your way, but leave their heavy burden behind and skip ahead toward your future.

....

....

....

"DON'T YOU CARRY
STONES IN YOUR
BOWL OF LIGHT."

—"BOWL OF LIGHT," TREVOR HALL

FROM GAG TO GIGGLES

Make a list of a few of the things that have bothered you recently. They can be life crises, pet peeves, or little frustrations that are generally benign but make you want to hurl.

....

....

....

....

....

Cross that shit out! Make a list of your favorite belly-laugh moments, your favorite jokes, or the funniest thing someone has said to you recently.

....

....

....

....

....

....

DO WHAT YOU CAN
TO MAKE LIFE NOT SUCK

Not everyone wakes up with the sun shining on their face, with cheerful songbirds laying out their clothing, or with golden opportunities resting at their feet. Sometimes it's all you can muster to get out of bed.

But, guess what? It's a new day! Hop the fuck out from underneath those covers. Whether it's something large or small, what are some ways you can make your world a better place to be?

"ANYTHING
IS POSSIBLE
IF YOU'VE
GOT ENOUGH
NERVE."

*—HARRY POTTER AND
THE HALF-BLOOD PRINCE,
J.K. ROWLING*

Well, maybe not anything. Becoming supremely good at sword juggling when you have issues with spatial reasoning is dubious at best, just as seeing six figures drop into your bank account for no reason is statistically unlikely. But that doesn't mean you shouldn't give your goals a shot. What are some things that you've been working up the nerve to do or to try?

MONTH OF FUCK, YES!

Make your next month a little more interesting. When you would ordinarily say "no" to something because you were too tired, too nervous, or too [*Reasons!*], try to say "yes" instead.* What fun opportunities or social settings can you open up by jumping right in? Make a note of them here, and how you felt afterward.

Except the unsafe things. Don't do those.

LET'S DO THIS!

1. ....
2. ....
3. ....
4. ....
5. ....
6. ....
7. ....
8. ....
9. ....
10. ....
11. ....
12. ....
13. ....
14. ....
15. ....

16. ....
17. ....
18. ....
19. ....
20. ....
21. ....
22. ....
23. ....
24. ....
25. ....
26. ....
27. ....
28. ....
29. ....
30. ....

SYMBOLISM!

Putting a message in a bottle, scattering ashes from a mountaintop, ~~slashing a couple of tires~~... Sometimes visual representations of saying farewell to the shit that plagues you can be really helpful. What kind of healthy acts of symbolism can you use to shut the door on something that's been bothering you?

_____

_____

_____

_____

_____

_____

_____

_____

_____

_____

Put your woes in a box, wrap it in a pretty fucking ribbon, and put it on your emotional shelf. Keep it there as a gift of experience from your life. Don't let it be a creepy-ass Jack-in-the-box that keeps opening back up on you.

SPIN CYCLE

The world spins pretty damn fast, and it can be easy to get caught up in the whirlwind of things to do and stress about. If you're the type of person who feels guilty just staying in bed past your alarm, not having a jam-packed schedule, or not moving at a speedy clip all fucking day—take a breather. The next time you feel this urge, halt that terrestrial rotation and let the stress move around you.

How can you take a moment to slow the hell down?

....

....

....

....

....

....

....

....

How can you make a habit of it?

....

....

....

....

....

....

....

CAN'T SPELL "CATHARTIC" WITHOUT "ART," AMIRIGHT?!

Write down the negatives of something that brings you some serious fucking frustration, and the positives of something that brings you joy. Fill the blank page at right. Then, using dark markers, stickers, washi tape, or some fancy glitter, cover up the spaces with all of the negative words.

CHECK IT OUT! Your abstract art is pretty as fuck. Let the positive vibes from the art you've created be a reminder that beauty can come from ugliness if you give it the right kind of attention.

LISTENING SKILLS!

Your kindergarten teacher was right. Listening is important!
List a few times when someone didn't listen to you and
describe how it made you feel.

....

....

....

....

....

....

Wanna bet you've done the same thing? Take a moment
to consider whether you need to STFU when someone is
speaking to you. How can you be a better listener?

....

....

....

....

....

....

A SPOONFUL OF
SHUT THE FUCK UP
HELPS THE MEDICINE
GO DOWN

RAINBOWS FOR DAYZ

Life isn't all sunny skies. It's dark clouds, it's lightning, it's a windy fucking cyclone of things you can't control. But the beauty of this combination of sunshine, water, and wind is the rainbow that emerges. On this cloudier side of the page, write down some of the difficult things in your life. On the sunny side, write some of the brighter things. Next to the little rainbow, write the positive results of this colorful little friendship between the sun and the clouds.

"THE SOUL SHOULD
ALWAYS STAND AJAR,
READY TO WELCOME THE
ECSTATIC EXPERIENCE."

—EMILY DICKINSON

OPEN YOUR HEART AND YOUR BLACK, BLACK SOUL

Closing yourself off to opportunities and relationships is bad. We know this. The physical act alone gives you bad posture. So, sit up a little straighter, or open that door a crack. How can you keep yourself ajar to new things in small ways?

"I ALWAYS WANTED TO BE SOMEBODY, BUT NOW I REALIZE I SHOULD HAVE BEEN MORE SPECIFIC."

—LILY TOMLIN

Make a list of your personal characteristics—the ones that make you feel shitty, the ones that make you feel fucking great, and the ones you'd like to have one day.

....

....

....

....

....

....

Circle the ones you're aiming for. How can you use the ones that make you feel great to get to the ones you're aiming for?

....

....

....

....

....

....

PEACE AND
FUCKING QUIET

Get rid of your noise pollution. What kind of annoying-as-fuck distractions are making their way into your senses?

....

....

....

....

....

....

Take a moment to drown out the noise. What thoughts go through your head when you let the quiet take over?

....

....

....

....

....

....

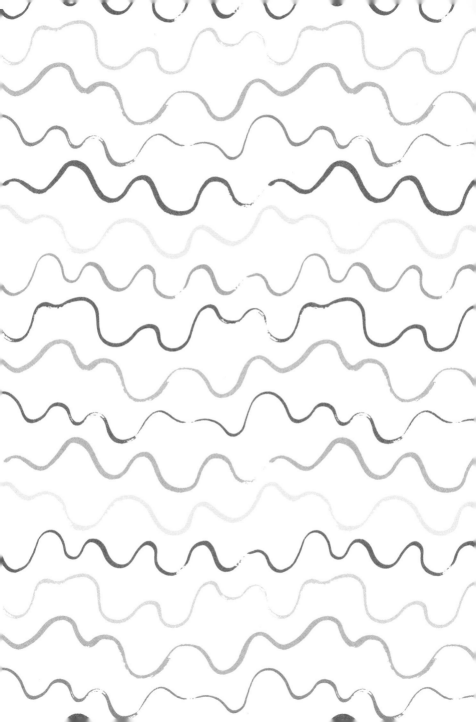

NAMAST'AY RIGHT HERE

What are the stressful things that keep you running around like a frenzied but high-functioning toddler?

....

....

....

....

Let yourself have a day, an evening, or even an hour to stop what you're doing and let yourself be your grown-ass self. Hang on the couch, sit outside, meditate, or do whatever makes you feel relaxed as fuck. What will you do?

....

....

....

....

How does it feel to let the stressful stuff pass you by?

....

....

....

....

83

MOOD RINGS A BELL

Label the colors on this page with the different moods that resonate with you. Skip words like "happy" or "sad," and instead use words or phrases that actually encompass your feelings, even if they're non-traditional or don't mean a damn thing to anyone but you (e.g., *amazeballs*, *MURDER*, *Sunday scaries*, and *Eeyore* are all perfectly acceptable entries).

Which of these moods is your favorite, and which one sucks the most?

....

....

....

....

....

....

Is there anything you can do to lessen a dark mood's hold on you?

....

....

....

....

....

....

....

RADICAL RORSCHACH

Check out this sweet ink blot! Without thinking, write the
words or ideas that pop into your head. Go!

....

....

....

....

....

....

What do they mean to you?

....

....

....

....

....

....

HAPPY HAPPY JOY JOY

Where can you go that will bring you a whole bunch of happy? Is it an indoor venue, or an outdoor space? Whether it's a quiet corner, a public place, or a special chair that's comfy as fuck, make a list of your favorite spots. Pick some dates or times to make yourself go there and enjoy some happy, happy moments.

"TAKE ME SOMEPLACE
WHERE THERE'S MUSIC
AND THERE'S LAUGHTER."

—"MY SILVER LINING,"
FIRST AID KIT

GOLD STARS!

Rewarding good behavior to inspire more good behavior doesn't work on everyone (puppies and small children are such effing takers!), but it sure does help. Deleting voicemails you've been holding onto from an ex, taking a breath and letting frustration pass, or opting out of something you want to do but know you reaaally shouldn't are all small but brave acts that deserve recognition.

What are some things you should praise yourself for?

....

....

....

....

....

....

....

How can you reward yourself for these small victories and claim your own gold stars?

....

....

....

....

....

....

NEXT STOP,
TWILIGHT ZONE

LET'S GET HEADY. If you were to make up your own
reality, using your cool-as-fuck dimension of imagination,
what would you create?

....

....

....

How would this world be different from reality?

....

....

....

How could its twists and irregularities work in your favor?

....

....

....

PUT ON YOUR FLOATIES

Imagine you're floating on a river. The water is just
the right amount of cool, the sun is shining, and the
current is smooth. You've got on your sunnies and
you're feeling great. This lazy river doesn't give one
fuck. It'll go where it goes. It'll get there when it
gets there.

What thoughts come to mind as you float on down?

....

....

....

....

How does the meandering of the river make you feel?

....

....

....

....

Can you channel this feeling of no-fucks-given buoyancy to other situations? Which ones?

....

....

....

....

....

THE ANTI-ABYSS

Ruminating on things that bother you is sure to send you tumbling down a black hole of despair. Instead of getting swallowed up by that dark hole or bumping into debris on your way down, see if you can avoid the pit altogether or grab a rope to pull yourself back up. What ways can you pull yourself out of those dark moments? Make a list of activities or distractions that can help you avoid getting sucked in—even if it's just temporarily.

BUZZ OF INSPIRATION

What little bits of inspiration can you find fluttering
all around you? Whether it's the scenery in your
neighborhood, a line from a song, or finding out that
honeybees communicate by doing a "waggle dance," take
note of the things that surprise and inspire
you here. Go ahead, get waggly as fuck.

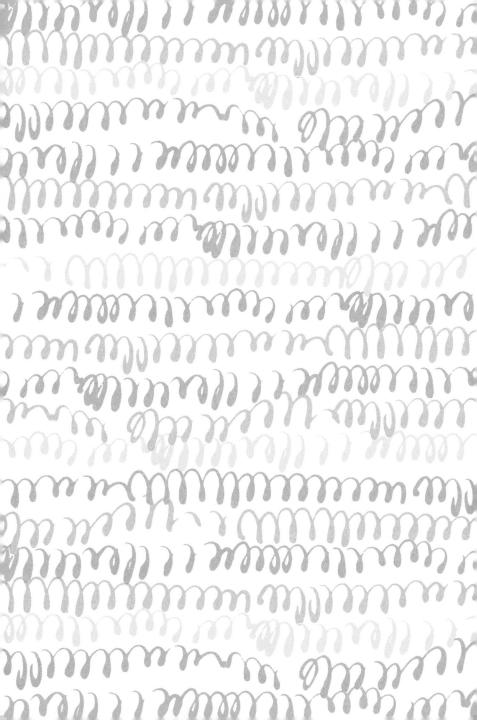

SWIPPY SWAPPY

Going cold-turkey on the activities and behaviors that aren't all that great for you isn't exactly easy. Bad habits are tricky as hell to break, but diversions definitely help. What are some tendencies that could easily be diverted by more positive behaviors?

HABIT		DIVERSIONS!
Unleashing unholy wrath via text message when angered.		*Pause. Look up some funny memes and send them to people who don't piss you off.*
Getting to the point where Netflix asks you if you're OK.		*Go for a walk, jaunt, or skip before pressing play.*

ROSÉ

WORDS THAT ARE HARD TO SAY ANGRILY

In times of blinding rage, take a deep breath. Let it out gently, and pull out your dictionary of delight. Say them aloud when you need them. Add your own!

HIPPOPOTAMUS

BUBBLES

SUNSHINE

VROOOM

GIGGLE

SPARKLE

TWINKLE

FLAMINGO

UPBEAT AF!

What's your happy playlist—the kind of music that makes you feel super fucking jazzed, optimistic, or otherwise invincible? Make a list of the songs or your favorite lyrics from the songs. Turn them way up when you need a boost.

PLOT TWIST

Every once in a while, our stories change out of fucking nowhere. Sometimes, these surprise turn of events ARE THE BEST KINDS OF SURPRISES, like unexpected visitors or free bottles of wine. Others feel more like a freight train barreling down the center of your life's hopes and dreams. For the ones somewhere in between, how can you find excitement or opportunity in this sudden change of plot? Make a storyboard of some of your own life's dramedies and how you'd like them to turn out.

1.

2.

3.

4.

5.

6.

IT'S NOT ALL ABOUT YOU, YA JERK!

Being a giant orb of sunshine in the center of your own universe isn't just about looking impressive. It's also about caring for everyone in your orbit—providing warmth, spreading a little light, and protecting your friends and family from your own massive supernovas of destruction. What are some ways you can spread your sunlight outward, rather than focus inward on your own starry self?

"EVEN IF YOU'RE
ON THE RIGHT TRACK,
YOU'LL GET RUN OVER
IF YOU JUST SIT THERE."
—WILL ROGERS

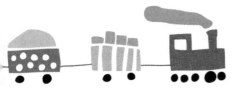

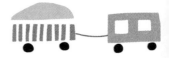

IMMOBILITY, BE DAMNED!

It's easy to get stuck. Whether it's a proverbial crossroads, a lack of momentum from your train being stuck in the green energy debate, or a pit of quicksand inexplicably obstructing your route, how can you get yourself moving again? What small steps can you take to move your fancy-ass steam engine forward?

SERENDIPITY-DOO-DAH

Make a little room for life's fortuitous surprises. What are some happy things, super-duper fun detours, or exciting plans you can enact to welcome something out of the ordinary? Get your happenstance happenin', now!

SPACE INVADERS!

Does your space—your bedroom, your cozy hangout, your favorite spot—reflect your present reality? Take a look around this space and see if you can tidy it the fuck up by removing relics of your past. Make a list of the things that reflect Old You and Now You.

OLD YOU	NOW YOU
....	....
....	....
....	....
....	....
....	....
....	....
....	....
....	....
....	....
....	....
....	....
....	....
....	....
....	....

Ditch the things that remind you of parts of your past
that aren't supporting the you as you are now, whether
by packing them in a box or shoving them out to
Deep Space.

THROW AWAY THE SPOON

Don't let yourself get trapped in a fucking category. What are the labels the people around you try to give you? How do they make you feel?

What are the many flavors of your personality that taste the best and the worst, that have the sharpest zing, that are subtle or sweet, or that give off the fieriest heat?

"I COME IN TOO MANY FLAVORS FOR ONE FUCKING SPOON."

—STACEYANN CHIN

IT'S ALREADY TOMORROW IN NEW ZEALAND

Such great news! The world is not ending! (Unless, of course, you live in New Zealand and you know something the rest of the world doesn't know.) On the days when it feels like the earth is coming off of its goddamn axis or the apocalypse is nigh, remember that there's sunshine on the horizon. What are some things in the coming days that you're looking forward to?

ZEN AS FUCK

Part of arriving in the peaceful zone found somewhere
between unencumbered rage and pure enlightenment
is being able to let go of the shit that bothers you.
It's not all going to go away in one fell swoop, and
some of it will never leave. Regardless, get a little
funky with your dysfunction, balance the things that
suck with things that give you true fucking joy, and
remind yourself that you're not alone on this tiny
planet zipping around the sun. What are the things
that make you feel most at peace, that help you let go,
and remind you that the best shit lies ahead?

ACKNOWLEDGMENTS

Sending my cheerful thanks to Aimee Chase, Katie Jennings Campbell, Marisa Bartlett, Tara Long, Jennifer Leight, Holly Schmidt, Allan Penn, and Bruce Lubin. To Andy Martin, Nichole Argyres, Courtney Littler, Amelie Littell, and the whole gang at St. Martin's for continuing to make the books we all like so much. Big hugs to Shelly Scarborough, Jamie Engstrom, and Rachel Pekarek for standing alongside all my favorite IDGAF endeavors.

MONICA SWEENEY is a writer and editor.
She lives in Boston, Massachusetts.